T0205023

Shaken Not Purred

Kitty-themed Cocktails for Cat Lovers

Jay Catsby

Contents

Classic Cattails

Based on the old fashioned, these straightforward drinks highlight the qualities of their base spirit.

Sour Puss

For those who love a citrusy drink, such as a margarita, these sour flavours are your go-to.

Furry Fizz

For those who are partial to something a little more bubbly.

Shorthair Varieties

Spirit-forward drinks (read strong). Those who like a negroni should love these.

The Purrfect Pairs

Duo and trio cocktails with two or three ingredients. For those who love a revolver or a White Russian.

Longhair Varieties

These are highball or long drinks that use tonic or soda. Refreshing cocktails such as a Tom Collins are found here.

Exotic Breeds

For more unconventional or complicated recipes, try this section.

Kittens' Mogtails

For those who can't or don't want to have an alcoholic drink, try this section.

Introduction

Hello, my feline-infatuated friends, and welcome to *Shaken Not Purred* – your definitive guide to all things cat and cocktail. If you've just picked up this book and are wondering if it's for you, let me do my best to sum up what follows.

This is no ordinary cocktail recipe book. It's a recipe book created specifically for the superior portion of the population who understand that man's best friend isn't some noisy, barking dog, but rather those cool, calm and chaotic creatures that love nothing better than sitting on your face at 3am, screaming until breakfast is served.

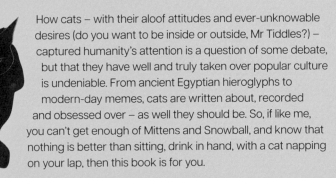

How cats – with their aloof attitudes and ever-unknowable desires (do you want to be inside or outside, Mr Tiddles?) – captured humanity's attention is a question of some debate, but that they have well and truly taken over popular culture is undeniable. From ancient Egyptian hieroglyphs to modern-day memes, cats are written about, recorded and obsessed over – as well they should be. So, if like me, you can't get enough of Mittens and Snowball, and know that nothing is better than sitting, drink in hand, with a cat napping on your lap, then this book is for you.

The book features over 60 cat-themed cocktail recipes, from variations on classic cattails to new and exciting recipes for those who are 'feline' adventurous. For novice kittens (those of age, of course) gently dipping their paws into the mixology world for the first time, this book offers a step-by-step guide to understanding the basics of cattails. Discover the tools you will need to create a mouthwatering Meowgarita, learn the difference between a 'longhair' and 'sour puss' cocktail, and try experimenting with exotic ingredients from all over the world. For more experienced moggies, this book contains variations on well-loved cocktail recipes, pro tips on how to layer drinks and express oils from citrus peels, and new and unusual recipes based on the most popular cat breeds. Learn to prepare a drink like a true aristocat, and get inspired.

The recipes have been divided by cocktail type to make things a little easier if you're looking for a specific drink. Each chapter includes a variety of recipes featuring a range of base spirits and, where I can, I've designed the recipes to be as simple as possible to measure and make. Each recipe is for a single serving (unless otherwise stated) so they are easy to scale up, too. When you've got a pack of thirsty friends waiting for their drinks, measuring exact amounts feels like a faff, so almost every recipe uses increments of half, single or double shots. Where possible I've also listed alternatives or substitution options for any unusual spirits or ingredients. Cats, while snooty, are never pretentious, so these recipes are available to all.

There is no right way to use this book. Feel free to read it cover to cover, as it was written, or dip in and out, like a mischievous orange cat that has discovered a thoughtlessly discarded cardboard box. The recipes can be picked and chosen as you wish, but if you find yourself confused by any of the terminology or ingredients, try consulting the first few sections for guidance. And, as well as recipes and all the information you'll need on equipment and techniques, the book contains a host of surprising cat facts, famous kitten trivia, insight into cat breeds and more cat-centric information than you can shake a laser pointer at. I hope you enjoy trying these cat-themed drinks as much as I have enjoyed creating them, and that you will be purring in pleasure by the end of this book.

Equipment

If cocktail making is an art, then these are your paintbrushes. Knowing what key equipment you'll need and how it works isn't going to make you an instant mixology expert, but having the right tools is the surest way to be off to a good start. Below, I've listed the key pieces we'll be using in this book. While it may seem like a lot, you don't need every item to start making cattails. A cocktail shaker, jigger, bar spoon and Hawthorne strainer are a great starting point. As you expand your cocktail repertoire, you can add more specialized tools.

Cocktail shaker: The clue is in the name here. Used to literally shake ingredients together, a shaker helps to mix, chill and dilute the cattails. The most common types are the Boston shaker, which features two 'cans' or pieces (usually made from stainless steel) that fit together to form a watertight seal, and the cobbler shaker, which features a top with a large, inbuilt strainer and a cap for shaking.

Mixing glass: A large glass that can be used for cocktails that are prepared by stirring or mixing rather than shaking. You can buy a specific glass for this, and some work as the top half of a Boston-style cocktail shaker, but really any large glass will work.

Bar spoon: A bar spoon has a long, twisted handle for stirring ingredients in a mixing glass and for layering different liquors (see page 14 for more on this technique). Plus, it looks fancy when it gets stuck in your kitchen draw.

Jigger: This tool measures liquid. It's typically a double-sided hourglass shape, with a single shot (25ml/¾fl oz in the UK) on one side and a double shot (50ml/1½fl oz for the more mathematically challenged) on the other. Most of the recipes in this book use some combination of single, double and half (10ml/¼fl oz) shots to make your life a bit easier, and so you can get back to more important things, like drinking your cocktails or playing with your kitten.

Hawthorne strainer: This strainer fits onto a shaker tin (the bottom part of a cocktail shaker) or mixing glass to separate the ice and other solid ingredients, such as fruit or herbs, from the liquid when pouring into a glass.

Fine strainer: A fine strainer is used in addition to the Hawthorne strainer for cocktails that include ingredients like fresh juice, herbs or muddled fruit to remove any small pieces – key for people who don't like the 'pulpy bits' in their cocktails or juice.

Muddler: A muddler is a bartender's pestle, used to mash (or 'muddle') fruits, herbs and spices in the bottom of a glass to release their flavours. Usually made from wood.

Citrus juicer: Fresh citrus juice is a key ingredient in many cocktails. A hand-held citrus juicer ensures you can extract juice quickly and efficiently. There are many types, so pick the one you prefer. Pre-squeezed citrus juice is available for those feeling lazier than a Ragdoll on a hot Tuesday morning, but I wouldn't recommend it.

Channel knife/zester: This tool is used for cutting thin twists of citrus peel for garnishes. Should be sharp. Keep away from kittens.

Cocktail sticks: These are used for skewering garnishes like olives, cherries or cocktail onions.

Ice bucket and tongs: An ice bucket keeps ice cubes ready for use and tongs allow for sanitary ice handling. DO NOT put your glass directly into the ice bucket to scoop out ice.

Cutting board and knife: These are essential for cutting up garnishes and ingredients.

7

Glassware

There are lots of opinions about what glasses are required for which cocktails, but I'm here to tell you that, like cat breeds, glasses are 90 per cent aesthetic and won't fundamentally change your drinking experience. Sacrilege, I know, but this is actually great news. It means that you can choose the glass that best suits your look. So, if your fragile masculinity can't handle drinking from a martini glass, and you don't want to go to therapy, then a rocks glass will work just as well. That being said, the right glass can enhance the cocktail's taste, highlight its presentation and elevate the overall drinking experience, taking your cocktails from average to the cat's pyjamas. Below, I have explained they key glass types and why you might want to use them. As with cat breeds, there are many more types, sets and subsets of glassware to explore, but this list should keep you going for now.

Rocks (old fashioned) glass: This short, sturdy glass typically holds about 180–240ml (6–8fl oz/¾–1 cup) of liquid and is used for spirit-forward cocktails served over ice, like the old fashioned or the negroni. Great for building (making) short cocktails in the glass, the lack of a stem means holding the glass will quickly warm up the cocktail if you serve it 'up' (without ice).

Highball and collins glasses: These tall, straight-sided glasses are used for long drinks, typically spirit-and-soda cocktails, again with ice.

Why? Because they can generally hold more liquid, around 250–350ml (8½–12fl oz/1–1¼ cups). A highball glass tends to be shorter and wider than a collins glass, but the terms are often used interchangeably. Great for a Tom Collins, mojito or Bloody Mary.

Martini glass: If you're feline fancy, this is the glass for you. Characterized by its iconic 'V' shape, this glass is typically used for cocktails served 'up' (without ice) after being chilled, such as a martini or cosmopolitan. The stem prevents your hand from warming the cocktail as you drink. They vary in size.

Coupe glass: A stemmed glass with a wide, shallow bowl, this style is also often used for serving cocktails 'up', like daiquiris or sidecars. Coupes are also used for Champagne. The wide bowl allows for a greater surface area, which helps to release the aromas of the cocktail. Sour and citrusy cocktails are great in these.

Wine glass: Your bog standard, run-of-the-mill wine glass. The stem helps to keep the drink cold, while the curved shape and deeper bowl allows you to get the full aroma as you drink. Great for fizz or wine-based cocktails, or for knocking off the table when placed too close to the edge.

Shot glass: Used for shots or small, strong cocktails, it typically holds 50ml (1½fl oz) liquid.

Flute or Champagne glass: A tall, thin glass, primarily used for Champagne or other sparkling wines, but also fizz-based cocktails such as the French 75. Hold by the stem to keep the glass cold and to look fancy. Typically contains 180ml (6fl oz/¾ cup) liquid.

Margarita glass: This is a variant of the martini glass, with an extra-chonky rim that's perfect for coating in salt or sugar. Used for, shockingly, margaritas.

Hurricane glass: This tall, curvy glass is named after the hurricane cocktail, a rum-based concoction. It's often used for tropical and frozen drinks.

Key Ingredients

OK, on to the fun stuff. It's time to talk about what you will be using to make your purrfect cocktails. Much like a playful kitten that's decided that the cardboard box his new cat toy came in is far more exciting than the toy itself, cocktail ingredients are only limited by your imagination. However, in this book I've kept the list relatively simple to make the recipes as accessible as possible. Here are most of the ingredients you'll need to make any of the recipes in the following chapters. Each one plays a crucial role in making a truly clawsome cocktail. The spirits form the base; the liqueurs, bitters and vermouth add complexity; juices and syrups adjust sweetness and acidity; soda and tonic add volume; and garnishes provide the finishing touches. By understanding each element, you can explore, experiment and create your own delightful cocktails.

Spirits: The base of most cocktails, spirits provide the lion's share of the alcohol content and flavour. The main spirits used in this book are whiskey (including Scotch whisky, bourbon, rye and others), gin (London dry, Plymouth and others), vodka, rum (dark or light), tequila and brandy. Each spirit carries a distinct flavour profile, influencing the character of the cocktail.

Liqueurs: These are sweetened spirits, often used to add complexity and flavour to cocktails. Examples include, but are far from limited to, Baileys Irish Cream, Kahlúa, Grand Marnier, amaretto and Cointreau. They provide additional flavour profiles like coffee, cream, orange, almond and many, many more.

Bitters: Bitters are high-proof alcohol infusions that use various herbs, spices and botanicals. There are many types, including different regional-specific variations, but Angostura and Peychaud's are among the most famous. They're like the salt and pepper of cocktail-making, used in drops or dashes to enhance and balance other flavours. Experiment and see what works best with each recipe.

Vermouth: Created in the 19th century, vermouth is a type of aromatized wine. It comes in sweet (red) and dry (white) varieties, though different flavoured variations also exist. It's a key ingredient in many shorter cocktails. Note that because vermouth has a lower ABV (alcohol content) than spirits and is more like wine, it should be stored in the refrigerator once opened and used within a few weeks.

Juices: For those sour pusses who like a bit of acid, freshly squeezed citrus juices like lemon, lime, orange and grapefruit are often used to brighten and flavour cocktails. Pineapple and cranberry juices are also popular in tropical and fruit-forward cocktails.

Syrups: Used to sweeten and flavour cocktails, syrups come in many forms. The most common is simple syrup, which is a standard in many cocktail recipes. It's the best and easiest way to get sweetness into a cocktail without changing flavours or relying on sugar dissolving in a cold, concentrated mixture. It is very easy to make, but for those who haven't made it before, below is a simple recipe. I recommend making a large batch and storing this for use in future cattails. It will last for about 2 months before it starts to become cloudy. Other types of syrups such as grenadine, agave nectar or flavoured syrups, like vanilla or ginger, can also add unique flavours.

Ingredients
500ml (17fl oz/generous 2 cups) water
500g (1lb 2oz/2¼ cups) granulated sugar

Instructions
1. Heat the water in a saucepan over a medium heat until simmering.

2. Add the sugar and stir until fully dissolved.

3. Remove from the heat and allow to cool, then transfer to an airtight container and store in the refrigerator.

Soda and tonic water: These carbonated beverages are often used as mixers to add volume and effervescence (aka fizz) to cocktails. Tonic water also contains quinine, adding a bitter flavour that pairs well with gin.

Egg whites: Used in drinks such as the whiskey sour and pisco sour, egg whites give a frothy or creamy texture to cocktails. Ever wanted to try a soufflé cocktail? Just add egg white and 'dry shake' (see page 14) for 3–5 minutes, or until your arms get tired. Egg whites don't affect the taste of a cocktail, but we wouldn't recommend them if you're pregnant, even in alcohol-free cocktails.

Cream: Cream is used in trio cocktails like the White Russian or brandy Alexander to provide a rich, smooth texture and to mellow stronger flavours. Just don't let your furry friend nab it when making your drink.

Fruits and herbs: Garnishes like citrus twists, fresh berries, mint sprigs or maraschino cherries can add visual appeal, aroma and a hint of flavour to the finished drink. Other types of fruit and herb, such as raspberries or coriander (cilantro), are muddled into cocktail mixes to add flavour.

Ice: Is ice really an ingredient, you ask? Well, unless you like drinking lukewarm straight gin, then ice is crucial in cocktails. It chills, dilutes and helps to mix ingredients. The size and shape of ice can impact the dilution rate and temperature of the cocktail. The main types are ice cubes (used for mixing and to chill many types of drinks), crushed ice (like normal ice if it had just received some really bad news at work) and oversized ice cubes (large ice cubes made with a speciality mould, which are great for drinks like old fashioneds or negronis that you want to dilute more slowly).

Pro Tips

So, you have the equipment, the ingredients and the desire. Maybe your cocktail experience is limited to gin and tonics and vodka lemonades, or maybe you're an expert. Either way, there are a few tips and tricks that can help make your next catcoction the best it pawsibily can be.

Be a picky puss – quality matters: Cocktails are only as good as their lowest-quality ingredient. This is doubly true for spirit-forward and short drinks. Your fur baby wouldn't accept low-quality chow, and you shouldn't use low-quality spirits, either.

Shaken or stirred – when and how to shake cocktails: The most common process for mixing cocktails is to shake them with ice. This vigorously mixes the cocktail ingredients together and rapidly chills them. To shake, put your ingredients into a cocktail shaker with plenty of ice and then firmly add the lid. Hold the top and bottom of the cocktail shaker in each hand to ensure that it doesn't come apart, and then shake hard.

An extra shake – dry shaking: Dry shaking is when you shake a cocktail without ice first. You do this with cocktails that contain egg white in order to emulsify the egg and add air to the mixture, creating a creamy, foamy drink.

Stripes like a tabby – layering cocktails: Want to layer your cocktails like a pro? Use an upturned cocktail spoon. The spirals down the length of a cocktail spoon are specifically designed to help you pour and layer liquids onto or under each other. To layer or 'float' a drink, turn your cocktail spoon and, holding it by the bowl, place the bottom into the drink at the height of the next layer you'd like to pour (usually this is just on top of the previous layer). Pour the next liquid very slowly against the bowl of the upturned spoon, letting it flow down the spoon and into the cocktail. You'll be making tiger stripes in no time.

Coming unstuck – getting a cocktail shaker separated: Cocktail shakers are great, but they do sometimes have a habit of getting stuck together as they are cooled by ice. To open a cocktail shaker, don't hit it against the side of your counter. Place the edge of the shaker, just below the join, against the side of something stable. Using the leverage this gives you, push the top of the shaker away from you to create an angle and release the shaker along one edge. The rest should come off easily.

Getting the zoomies – how to 'express' citrus: Expressing citrus peel or rind is a method of extracting the essential oils and aromas of the fruit without adding sweetness or sourness to the body of the cocktail. It also makes you look like a pro. To do it, cut a thin oval from the skin of a fresh fruit (usually an orange, lemon or lime), avoiding cutting too deep into the pith. Squeeze the fruit between thumb and forefinger or twist with two hands over the cocktail. If you've got sharp eyes, you may see some oil squirt out of the peel onto the cocktail. You can garnish with the peel or discard it.

Chilly kitty – chilling your glasses: Chilling a glass is recommended for cocktails that are served up without ice. You can either pop the glass into the refrigerator 30 minutes before making the cocktail or fill the glass you're about to use with ice and leave it to sit for 5 minutes before emptying and filling with the cocktail.

Purrfect rims – getting your salt and sugar rims right: Consistently rimmed glasses make a big difference to the taste and presentation of many cocktails. Here's how to do it: run some citrus around the edge of the glass you'd like to rim. Next, place your chosen ingredient (salt, sugar, etc.), into a glass or wide, flat dish. Press the outside rim of the glass into the mixture, rotating it around until the rim is evenly coated. Try not to get any on the inside of the glass where it could fall into the cocktail.

Classic Cattails

Classic cattails are one of the simplest forms of cocktail. They are sometimes known as 'ancestral' cocktails because they were some of the first mixed drinks created in the 19th century. They consist mainly of a base spirit, mixed with a sweetener and usually a bitters to add flavour, and are generally served on the rocks (in a short glass with ice). As their flavour is heavily dependent on the quality of the spirt used, don't skimp on these cocktails. These recipes are simple, straightforward, strong and, when made correctly, extremely tasty.

Old Furrshioned

A classic among classics, any cattail aficionados should recognize this recipe.
I recommend bourbon as the classic choice for this drink, but feel free to experiment with
your favourite whiskeys to see how they taste. The trick here is to stir the drink well, both
to cool it and to dilute the cocktail to your preferred strength.

Ingredients

1 sugar cube
3 dashes of Angostura bitters
75ml (2½fl oz) whiskey (bourbon is the classic choice)
Lemon twist, to garnish

Instructions

1. Place the sugar cube in a rocks glass and add the bitters.
2. Using a muddler, crush and grind the sugar cube.
3. Add an oversized ice cube to the glass, then pour
in the whiskey.
4. Using a bar spoon, stir until the sugar has dissolved,
the outside of the glass is cool to the touch and the
cattail is diluted to your desired strength.
5. Garnish with the lemon twist.

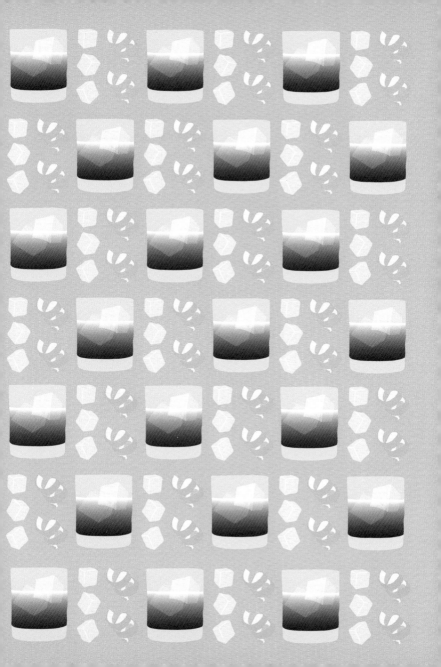

Tiddles

Navy-strength rum refers to any rum with an ABV (alcohol by volume) of more than 57 per cent. Historically, rum and gunpowder were stored together below decks on Royal Navy vessels. Sometimes the rum would leak out and soak into the gunpowder, so the rum had to be over 57 per cent to ensure that the gunpowder would still explode when lit. This cattail is named after one of the most well-travelled professional sailor cats who kept Royal Navy aircraft carriers free of mice. I've included a lime garnish in reference to the limes that British sailors used to eat to help stave off scurvy.

Ingredients

75ml (2½fl oz) navy-strength rum
Dash of Bittercube Jamaican No. 1 Bitters (or regular bitters)
10ml (¼fl oz) rich demerara syrup (see below)
Lime twist, to garnish

For the rich demerara syrup
150ml (5fl oz/scant ⅔ cup) water
300g (10½oz/1⅓ cups) demerara sugar

Instructions

1. First, make the demerara syrup. Heat the water in a saucepan over a medium heat until simmering.

2. Add the sugar and stir until fully dissolved.

3. Remove from the heat and allow to cool, then transfer to an airtight container and store in the refrigerator.

4. Put three cubes of ice into a rocks glass, then add the rum, bitters and syrup.

5. Using a bar spoon, stir until the outside of the glass is cool to the touch and the cattail is diluted to your desired strength.

6. Finish with the lime twist.

Le Chat-zerac

Based on the 'official' cocktail of New Orleans, the sazerac, this variation on an old fashioned features a fun and lethal twist: a rinse of absinthe, the spirit that can be up to 75 per cent ABV and was famously banned in much of Europe and America in the 20th century. Its reputation has been overplayed, however, mainly due to its association with bohemian culture, and the drink is no more dangerous than other spirits. Some claim the sazerac is the oldest known American cocktail, and in honour of that, I've embraced the French culture of New Orleans when naming this cattail. Traditionally, Cognac (a type of brandy) is used for this drink, but variations also use other brandies or rye whiskey. Try a few and see which you prefer.

Ingredients

5ml (1 teaspoon) absinthe
1 sugar cube
Dash of Peychaud's bitters
75ml (2½fl oz) brandy or rye whiskey

Instructions

1. Pour the absinthe into a chilled rocks glass. Swirl the glass to 'rinse' the inside of the glass, then discard the remaining absinthe.

2. Add the sugar cube and the bitters.

3. Using a muddler, crush and grind the sugar cube.

4. Add crushed ice and the whiskey.

5. Using a bar spoon, stir until the sugar has dissolved, the outside of the glass is cool to the touch and the cattail is diluted to your desired strength.

As well as being the birthplace of this classic cattail, New Orleans is home to a peculiar late-night feline hangout spot. Every evening, after the gates are locked, the Place d'Armes within Jackson Square Gardens is taken over by hundreds of mysterious moggies out on the prowl.

Oaxacat

The Oaxacat, inspired by the so-called 'tequila old fashioned' from the Mexican town of Oaxaca, is a smoky twist on the famous whiskey-based drink. Technically, tequila is a form of mezcal, which is any agave-based spirit (tequila is made only from blue agave). However, mezcal is commonly known for its smoky taste, so it adds an interesting flavour to this cocktail. Please, please, please, don't use 'shooting' or run-of-the-mill tequila for this cocktail. Many types of tequila are made for sipping, just like whiskeys. It's well worth investing if you're thinking of giving this cocktail a try.

Ingredients

50ml (1½fl oz) tequila
25ml (¾fl oz) mezcal (or more tequila)
10ml (¼fl oz) agave nectar
Bittermens Xocolatl Mole Bitters (or regular bitters), to taste

Instructions

1. Fill a rocks glass with ice, then add the tequila, mezcal, agave nectar and bitters.
2. Using a bar spoon, stir until the outside of the glass is cool to the touch and the cattail is diluted to your desired strength.

Larry

While not the longest resident of 10 Downing Street, Larry (aka the Chief Mouser) has outlasted many a prime minister. Born in 2007, Larry began his tenure in 2011 after he was adopted from Battersea Dogs and Cats Home by the staff of Number 10. He still serves to this day, helping to keep the mice in check and the PMs humble. While the second task may be harder than the first, I'm confident that no one could be doing a better job. He outlasted his colleague, Palmerston, who was Chief Mouser in the Foreign Office until 2020. Because of his amazing work, I've decided to dedicate this most British cocktail to Larry. Featuring London dry gin and Angostura bitters, you're sure to get a flavour of the capital. Keep up the good work, Larry.

Ingredients

75ml (2½fl oz) London dry gin
10ml (¼fl oz) Simple Syrup (see page 12)
3 dashes of Angostura bitters
Lemon twist and juniper berries, to garnish

Instructions

1. Put an oversized ice cube into a chilled rocks glass, then add the gin, syrup and bitters.
2. Using a bar spoon, stir until the outside of the glass is cool to the touch and the cattail is diluted to your desired strength.
3. Garnish with the lemon twist and juniper berries.

Sour
Puss

Sour cocktails include some of the most famous and well-known cocktails in the world (think margarita and whiskey sour). Made with a base spirit that is mixed with citrus juice (usually lemon or lime) and syrups to sweeten, these crowd-pleasers know how to get a party started. As I've mentioned before, I'd recommend squeezing your own citrus where possible, in the same way that I'd recommend not trying to stroke your cat's tummy unless you want to risk your cute kitten opening an artery. If you must use pre-squeezed citrus, adjust the recipes to taste as not all pre-squeezed juices have the same strength or acidity. I've included exact amounts of citrus juice here, but as each lemon and lime is different, don't worry too much about using totally perfect amounts. Not so fun fact: citrus juice is actually toxic to cats, though generally only in larger amounts than they would ever eat or drink. Watch out with those used citrus peels.

Meowgarita

No cattail book would be complete without a variation on this classic. A famous choice for poolside drinks and poor choices worldwide, if you haven't at least heard of this cocktail before, you've probably been living under a rock with about 20 cats. Variations on this drink include serving it with or without salt, on the rocks, frozen or straight up. The version below is my personal favourite, and probably the most classic version of the cocktail, but hey, you're an independent person, so do what you want. For those who want to know the 'correct' way to rim a glass with salt, see page 15.

Ingredients

50ml (1½fl oz) tequila
25ml (¾fl oz) fresh lime juice (from about 1 lime)
10ml (¼fl oz) Cointreau (or other orange liqueur)
Flaky sea salt, to garnish
Lime wheel cut into the shape of a cat's face, to garnish

Instructions

1. Rim a martini glass with salt, being careful to only coat the outside.
2. Half-fill a cocktail shaker with ice and add the tequila, lime juice and Cointreau.
3. Shake until well chilled, then strain into the prepared glass.
4. Garnish with the lime wheel.

Whiskers Sour

Our first egg white cattail. Egg white is used in cocktails to create a silky-smooth texture, like a Persian cat's coat, without affecting flavour. This texture is brought about when the fats in the egg white emulsify to form a meringue-like texture. With its velvety texture, the sour hit from the lemon juice and the kick from the whisky, you'd be hard pressed to find a more sophisti-cat-ed cocktail anywhere.

Ingredients

50ml (1½fl oz) bourbon
25ml (¾fl oz) fresh lemon juice (from about 1 lemon)
10ml (¼fl oz) Simple Syrup (see page 12)
1 medium egg white
1 maraschino cherry, to garnish

Instructions

1. Combine the bourbon, lemon juice, simple syrup and egg white in a cocktail shaker (without ice).
2. Shake vigorously for 3–5 minutes until it forms a thick, foamy emulsion.
3. Add a scoop of ice and shake again until well chilled.
4. Using a Hawthorne strainer, strain the mixture into a rocks glass.
5. Garnish with the cherry.

Pawsco Sour

Pisco is made in the wine-making regions of Peru and Chile by distilling fermented grape juice in a similar way to brandy. This popular cattail combines smooth textures with refreshing lime juice, making for a great flavour - it is a pawsonal favourite of mine. If you're looking to make this cocktail extra authentic, and why wouldn't you, you can use Peruvian or Key limes, which are smaller and sweeter than their more common cousins. For an extra-smooth finish, shake the cocktail like an energetic kitten playing with a string toy.

Ingredients

50ml (1½fl oz) pisco
25ml (¾fl oz) fresh lime juice (from about 1 lime)
10ml (¼fl oz) Simple Syrup (see page 12)
1 medium egg white
Dash of Angostura bitters

Instructions

1. Combine the pisco, lime juice, simple syrup and egg white in a cocktail shaker (without ice).

2. Shake vigorously for 3–5 minutes until it forms a thick, foamy emulsion.

3. Add a scoop of ice and shake again until well chilled.

4. Using a Hawthorne strainer, strain the mixture into a chilled rocks glass.

5. Finish with a few drops of Angostura bitters.

The Nazca lines of Peru have been a source of fascination (and alien conspiracy theories) since their discovery in 1926. These ancient geoglyphs, which include an orca, monkey and hummingbird, were sketched into the earth thousands of years ago, for reasons unknown. In 2020, a new figure was unearthed that just proves the enduring popularity of our feline friends – that's right, a very cute-looking cat.

Grumpy Cat

This cattail is sure to give you a sour expression. Based on a gimlet and inspired by the internet-famous perpetually dissatisfied cat, it is purrfect for those who love sharp flavours. The gimlet has an interesting history. It was inspired by sailors (those boys sure love a drink) who, to avoid catching scurvy, would eat limes and lemons. Ships' captains found that the sour fruits went down a lot better when added to a bit of gin, and so the gimlet was born. Our slightly more refined version is great for anyone who enjoys sour sweets (candies) or hanging out with their mother-in-law.

Ingredients

75ml (2½fl oz) gin
50ml (1½fl oz) lime juice (from about 2 limes)
25ml (¾fl oz) Simple Syrup (see page 12)

Instructions

1. Half-fill a cocktail shaker with ice and add the gin, lime juice and simple syrup.
2. Shake until well chilled, then strain into a chilled coupe glass.

Ameowretto Sour

Amaretto is a sweet Italian liqueur generally flavoured with almonds or cherry stones. The sweetness makes it great for offsetting the citrus in a traditional sour. As amaretto is sugary enough as it is, I have left out the simple syrup, otherwise this cattail is at risk of over-sweetening. If you really can't enjoy it without a bit more sweetness, I'd recommend adding simple syrup a dash (5ml/1 teaspoon) at a time until you're happy. Too much will turn this cocktail into a cat-astrophe.

Ingredients

50ml (1½fl oz) amaretto
25ml (¾fl oz) fresh lemon juice (from about 1 lemon)
1 medium egg white
1 maraschino cherry, to garnish
Orange slice cut into the shape of a cat's face, to garnish

Instructions

1. Combine the amaretto, lemon juice and egg white in a cocktail shaker (without ice).
2. Shake vigorously for 3–5 minutes until it forms a thick, foamy emulsion.
3. Add a scoop of ice and shake again until well chilled, then use a Hawthorne strainer to strain the mixture into a chilled rocks glass.
4. Garnish with the cherry and orange slice.

Clawsmopolitan

This cattail is a sweeter take on the traditional sour cocktail that is loved all over the world for its bright pink colour and refreshing taste. The sharper of you may already recognize this cocktail from the iconic show *Sex and the City*. At least three people claim to have invented the original drink this is based on, but whoever was the first to combine cranberry juice with vodka, we salute you. I can imagine some very sophisticated cats and kittens sipping this on a tropical beach, in a fancy hotel suite or in a Manhattan bar somewhere.

Ingredients

50ml (1½fl oz) vodka
10ml (¼fl oz) Cointreau (or other orange liqueur)
10ml (¼fl oz) fresh lime juice (from about ½ lime)
25ml (¾fl oz) cranberry juice
Lime twist shaped like a cat's tail, to garnish

Instructions

1. Half-fill a cocktail shaker with ice and add the vodka, Cointreau, lime juice and cranberry juice.

2. Shake until well chilled, then strain into a chilled martini glass.

3. Garnish with the lime twist.

Pawloma

Loving these sour cattails but looking for something a bit longer to get your fuzzy mitts around? Look no further than the Pawloma. Possibly the most refreshing drink in this book, the mixture of lime juice, grapefruit juice and soda water makes this a real thirst quencher. Purrfect for a hot day when you need to cool down. The chilli and salt rim around the glass also gives this cattail a delicious kick, just to keep you on your toes.

Ingredients

50ml (1½fl oz) tequila
25ml (¾fl oz) fresh lime juice (from about 1 lime)
Pinch of flaky sea salt, plus extra to garnish
Grapefruit juice, to top
Soda water, to top
Chilli (hot pepper) flakes, to garnish
Grapefruit wheel, to garnish

Instructions

1. Combine a few pinches of salt and chilli flakes in a glass or small plate and rim a tall or highball glass with the mixture, then fill with ice to chill.
2. Half-fill a cocktail shaker with ice and add the tequila, lime juice and salt.
3. Shake until well chilled, then strain into the ice-filled glass.
4. Top with equal parts grapefruit juice and soda water, then stir with a bar spoon to combine.
5. Garnish with the grapefruit wheel.

Te-squeeler Sour

A variation on the Whiskers Sour (see page 32) for those who prefer their spirits Central rather than North American. When making this cattail, we're looking for a layer of foam that floats on top of the cattail. Think of a cat's topcoat and undercoat. The topcoat (the foam) sits on top, looking decorative and beautiful, while the undercoat (the rest of the cattail) does the main job of keeping your furry friend warm. Same here. Remember to drip a few drops of bitters into the foam for a really professional look.

Ingredients

50ml (1½fl oz) tequila
25ml (¾fl oz) fresh lemon juice (from about 1 lemon)
10ml (¼fl oz) Simple Syrup (see page 12)
1 medium egg white

To garnish
1 maraschino cherry
Lemon wheel
Angostura bitters

Instructions

1. Combine the tequila, lemon juice, simple syrup and egg white in a cocktail shaker (without ice).

2. Shake vigorously for 3–5 minutes until it forms a thick, foamy emulsion.

3. Add a scoop of ice and shake again until well chilled, then use a Hawthorne strainer to strain the mixture into a chilled rocks glass.

4. Garnish with the cherry and lemon wheel, then finish with a few drops of bitters.

Clover Claw

This silky-smooth cocktail was a favourite in the pre-prohibition era bars of Philadelphia. Reminiscent of a gimlet, the added raspberry syrup and egg white gives this cattail a delicious fruity flavour and smooth texture. While technically the egg white is optional in all cocktails, I'd strongly recommend you use it in this recipe as it's doing a key job of offsetting the sour components and providing the soufflé body, like a lovely chonky kitten. For those who can't find raspberry syrup and don't want to make their own, an alternative is to muddle 3-4 raspberries with 25ml (¾fl oz) Simple Syrup (see page 12) in the bottom of the shaker before mixing the cocktail.

Ingredients

50ml (1½fl oz) gin
25ml (¾fl oz) raspberry syrup
10ml (¼fl oz) fresh lemon juice (from about ½ lemon)
1 medium egg white
A few raspberries, to garnish

Instructions

1. Combine the gin, raspberry syrup, lemon juice and egg white in a cocktail shaker (without ice).

2. Shake vigorously for 3–5 minutes until it forms a thick, foamy emulsion.

3. Add a scoop of ice and shake again until well chilled, then use a Hawthorne strainer to strain the mixture into a chilled coupe glass.

4. Garnish with the raspberries.

Competitive Kittens

You're hosting a cat-themed cocktail party. Well, congratulations. You're already off to a great start by purchasing this book. But other than whipping up whatever favourite cattail your friends are feline, how else to keep your house guests entertained? Why not try a cat board game? Purrfect for every size of gathering.

Cat Lady: Play as a cat lady trying to collect the most cats possible (obviously a great idea). Draw cards featuring treats and tools such as cat nip or string toys, then use them to please your kittens and stop them from wandering off. Think you know how to manage your cats well enough to build your mini-menagerie? Or will it all end up being an exercise in herding cats?

Isle of Cats: This game sees you and your friends travelling to the long-lost 'Isle of Cats', where your mission is to save as many cats as possible before the evil Lord Vesh arrives. Explore the history of the island, find secret treasure and fill your boat with as many unique cat cards as possible while keeping the feline families together.

Purrlock Holmes: This guessing game invites you to play as master cat detectives, guessing the identities of various cat criminals. Use your skills of deduction to guess the traits of your suspects while your friends do the same. Are you smart enough to get a pawsitive identification or will the evil mastermind, Furriarty, escape?

Exploding Kittens: This classic has you and friends working your way through a deck of hilariously named kittens, trying to avoid being the ones to...well, explode. Let the tension mount as the deck shrinks, prepare your defence with Special-Ops Bunnies and the All-Seeing Goat, and hope you draw a Tacocat rather than the Exploding Kitten.

Schrödinger's Cats: This bluffing game will have you answering that famous thought experiment once and for all: is the cat alive or dead? Take on the role of a cat physicist, such as Albert Felinestine, Sally Prride or Neil deGrasse Tabby, and use your deductive skills (and your best poker face) to prove your hypothesis and keep everyone else in the dark.

Furry Fizz

This chapter is for those who are partial to something a little more bubbly. From drinks frequently found at a boozy brunch to those enjoyed as a sophisticated pre-evening tipple, all these cattails centre around Champagne or prosecco. If you like a mimosa or a French 75, you will love these recipes. I've recommended my preferred fizz option for each cattail, but most types of sparkling wine will work as a substitute, so feel free to swap out my suggestions with your favourite type of bubbles. For many of the cattails in this chapter I've also left the quantity of Champagne or prosecco up to you. The recipes are designed to be made in a standard Champagne flute or glass, but feel free to vary the amount of fizz depending on your preferences. Try filling some to the top and leaving others slightly more concentrated to see which flavour works best for you. Mixology is an art, not a science.

Now for some advice. I would avoid shaking any cocktails made with fizzy ingredients. Instead, gently stir these cattails to combine and pre-chill your ingredients and glasses in the refrigerator to keep everything cool.

Tea with a Tiger

Inspired by the wonderful children's book by Judith Kerr, once you've had one of these cattails, it's hard to stop. Don't say I didn't warn you. People have differing views on the right ratio of orange juice to Champagne for this cattail, but personally I like an equal-parts mix. If you want more Champagne, you can always make another one. If you're feeling like a tuxedo cat, and want to show off those fancy pants, try layering the orange juice and Champagne on top of each other with a bar spoon. The final effect should remind you of a tiger's stripes. It's tricky to get right, but I have faith in your steady paws.

Ingredients

75ml (2½fl oz) fresh orange juice
75ml (2½fl oz) Champagne
Orange twist, to garnish

Instructions

1. Using an upturned bar spoon, layer the Champagne and orange juice in alternating layers in a chilled Champagne glass (see page 14 for more on this method).
2. Garnish with the orange twist.

Apawrol Spritz

Does anything say summer like this cattail? Well, maybe lying on a warm patio and napping in the sun all day, but we can't all be cats, unfortunately. For those of us not lucky enough to be felines, an Apawrol Spritz is a close second. Aperol is an Italian aperitif, so I've chosen prosecco as the accompanying fizz for this cattail as its sweetness will best offset the bitter Aperol. Add a slice of orange to garnish, and this cattail is almost as Instagrammable as your cutest kitten. Can you get both the drink and the cat in the same shot? Ultimate like machine.

Ingredients

50ml (1⅔fl oz) Aperol
75ml (2½fl oz) prosecco
Splash of soda water
Orange slice, to garnish

Instructions

1. Fill a wine glass with ice, then add the Aperol and prosecco.

2. Top with the soda water, then stir with a bar spoon to combine.

3. Garnish with the orange slice.

Purrter
and Champagne

When someone first suggested this as a cattail, I have to admit I was sceptical.
How would the flavours of a porter beer offset the flavours of Champagne? The answer?
Deliciously. Those who don't like the coffee and toffee flavours of a porter may disagree,
but much like trying to find the right type of cat food for your household, you can't please
everyone. If you like a porter, I'd recommend giving this a go. This is another great chance
to show off your layering skills, as the different densities of the porter and Champagne
allow them to be separated if you pour carefully, creating a drink reminiscent of a tabby
cat's coat. Just make sure you paws long enough for the head on the beer to subside.

Ingredients

180ml (6 fl oz/¾ cup) porter
180ml (6 fl oz/¾ cup) Champagne

Instructions

1. Using an upturned bar spoon, layer the porter and
Champagne into a chilled wine or highball glass.

Raspberry Frisky

What's fancier than a glass of Champagne in a beautiful flute? A glass of pink Champagne with a delicious fresh raspberry, obviously. This cattail is really for those who want to dress to impress, so make sure you're wearing your best coat with this cattail. The lemon juice offsets the sweetness of the Chambord to create a delicious and refreshing drink.

Ingredients

10ml (¼fl oz) Chambord
10ml (¼fl oz) fresh lemon juice
Champagne, to top
A few raspberries, to garnish

Instructions

1. Combine the Chambord and lemon juice in a chilled Champagne glass and stir with a bar spoon.
2. Gently top with the Champagne, allowing the bubbles to subside before filling completely and allowing the colour of the Chambord to mix upwards.
3. Garnish with the raspberries.

Kitty Royale

While simple, this famous and sophisticated French cattail is great for anyone who's looking for a slight twist on traditional bubbles. Perhaps your surprise lottery win has left you feeling a bit bored of the 'everyday' stuff. Maybe you've discovered a crate of vintage Champagne in your mum's attic. Or maybe your cat has taken a dislike to Champagne bottles and you need to get them all out of the house as soon as possible. Whatever the reason, the colour from the blackcurrant liqueur and lemon twist really elevate this already delicious drink. Ooh la la!

Ingredients

10ml (¼fl oz) crème de cassis
Champagne, to top
Lemon twist shaped like a cat's tail, to garnish

Instructions

1. Combine the crème de cassis and Champagne in a chilled Champagne glass.
2. Top with the lemon twist.

Cat's Eye

Inspired by the beautiful golden colour of a playful kitten's eyes, this cocktail is another great summer drink. The sweetness from the limoncello offsets the bitterness of the Aperol to purrfection. Did you know cats' eyes reflect light because of a part called the *tapetum lucidum*. It's also responsible for giving them much better low-light vision than humans.

Ingredients

25ml (¾fl oz) limoncello
25ml (¾fl oz) Aperol
Prosecco, to top
Lemon wheel, to garnish

Instructions

1. Fill a wine glass with ice, then add the limoncello and Aperol.
2. Use a bar spoon to stir to combine, then top with the prosecco, allowing the ingredients to mix naturally.
3. Garnish with the lemon wheel.

*If you talk to
a dog or a cat it doesn't
tell you to shut up.*

Marilyn Monroe

Mitsou's Mixer

This cocktail is a variation on the Marylin Monroe, invented at New York's Waldorf Astoria hotel, near where Monroe filmed the iconic white dress subway grate scene for *The Seven Year Itch*. It features Champagne, purportedly Monroe's go-to beverage, with a twist. I've named it after her beautiful and beloved cat, Mitsou. She was the only cat that Marylin ever owned and was a beautiful white Persian.

Ingredients

100ml (3½fl oz) Champagne
25ml (¾fl oz) apple brandy
Dash of grenadine
2 maraschino cherries, skewered on a cocktail stick

Instructions

1. Pour the Champagne, apple brandy and grenadine into a chilled martini glass and stir to combine.

2. Garnish with the cherries.

Shorthair Varieties

In the late 18th century, some clever person refined the historic process of adding botanicals to wine and allowing it to ferment longer and stronger, thereby fortifying it. This created the modern recipe for vermouth. This development was great for many reasons, but it is particularly great for us as it opens up a whole new category of cattail - namely the short, or spirit-forward, cattail. Shorthair cattails consist of a 'primary spirit' mixed with a vermouth. They are some of the most popular cocktails ever created and should be built, not shaken. That means they are mixed in a glass over ice and stirred to allow a more precise control of the dilution. This also means you often don't need a cocktail shaker or strainer for these recipes, so they are great for beginners.

Short cattails are only as good as the ingredients you use. Combining low-quality gin with out-of-date vermouth isn't going to suddenly make either taste better. Trust your nose with this and don't be afraid to be picky. Channel your inner cat with a half-empty food bowl - you have standards.

Ne-groomi

The definition of a classic spirit-forward cattail. Also, the most popular cocktail
in the world according to numerous recent polls. The purrfect aperitif or pre-dinner drink,
this orange cocktail is only improved by expressing the orange twist before garnishing
the cattail (see page 15 for instructions on how to express citrus peel). For those who love
social media a little too much, don't get this confused with the negroni sbagliato (which
literally translates as a 'bungled' negroni). While also delicious, that's
not at all what we are going for here.

Ingredients

25ml (¾fl oz) gin
25ml (¾fl oz) Campari
25ml (¾fl oz) sweet vermouth
Orange twist shaped like a cat's tail, to garnish

Instructions

1. Put an oversized ice cube into a rocks glass and
add the gin, Campari and sweet vermouth.
2. Using a bar spoon, stir until the outside of the glass is cool
to the touch and the cattail is diluted to your desired strength.
3. Express the orange twist over the glass, then
use it to garnish.

Alley Cat
(the Purrfect Mancattan)

For the urbanites among you, it doesn't get more 'city' than this. There are many theories for the origin of this cattail, but my personal favourite is that the cocktail was invented in the Manhattan Club, New York, at a party hosted by Lady Randolph Churchill, mother of Winston Churchill. The Churchills, in particular Winston, were cat lovers and Winston had many pets during his lifetime including Micky, Tango, Nelson and Jock, a ginger cat gifted to him on his eighty-eighth birthday. When he moved into 10 Downing Street, he also inherited the cat of the former prime minister, Neville Chamberlain. The kitten was known as the 'Munich Mouser' in reference to Chamberlain's failed attempts at appeasement of Germany before the beginning of the Second World War.

Ingredients

60ml (2fl oz) rye whiskey
30ml (1fl oz) sweet vermouth
2 dashes of Angostura bitters
1 maraschino cherry, to garnish

Instructions

1. Half-fill a cocktail shaker with ice and add the whiskey, vermouth and bitters.

2. Shake until well chilled, then strain into a martini glass.

3. Garnish with the cherry.

Chartreux

This cattail gets its name from a rare breed of cat originally from France. Historically popular among the French aristocracy, this breed almost went extinct during the First and Second World Wars and is even now very rare. I think it is a fitting name to honour a very French cattail, based on the boulevardier. Traditionally a name for a wealthy gentleman or lady who prowled around the boulevards of Paris in search of revelry (sounds very cat-like to me), *Boulevardier* was also the name of a magazine written by this cattail's apparent inventor, Erskine Gwynne. Enjoy this classic drink while you strut around your home. I hope it brings you much revelry.

Ingredients

50ml (1½fl oz) bourbon
25ml (¾fl oz) sweet vermouth
25ml (¾fl oz) Campari
Orange twist, to garnish

Instructions

1. Half-fill a mixing glass with ice and add the bourbon, Campari and sweet vermouth.

2. Using a bar spoon, stir the mixture well.

3. Using a Hawthorne strainer, strain the mixture into a chilled coupe glass.

4. Express the orange twist over the glass, then use it to garnish.

Meowtini

Another true classic (this section is full of them), any mixologist worth her cat nip has their version. There is always a lot of debate about how much vermouth should be included in a martini. Not being a massive fan of straight gin myself, I've opted for a 'wetter' version here. Now, onto the controversial bit. Unless you drive an Aston Martin and work for British Intelligence, there is no excuse for shaking your Meowtinis. All this does is breaks up the ice, leaving ice shards and over-diluting the cattail. If you want this drink cold, and you do, I'd instead suggest freezing your glass before you make it.

Ingredients

50ml (1½fl oz) gin (or vodka)
10ml (¼fl oz) dry vermouth
Lemon twist, to garnish

Instructions

1. Fill a mixing glass with ice and add the gin and vermouth.

2. Using a bar spoon, stir the mixture well. DO NOT SHAKE.

3. Strain the mixture into a frozen martini glass.

4. Express the lemon twist over the glass, then use it to garnish.

Variation: Smelly Cat

For those who prefer their cattails a little less dry and a little more tangy, try a dirty martini. Add 10ml (¼fl oz) olive brine and 20ml (½fl oz) dry vermouth to the gin, then mix as above. Garnish with 3 olives speared on a cocktail stick.

Catnip Dreams

This green cattail was inspired by cats' favourite treat. The green colouring from the crème de menthe adds a unique look and the minty flavour is reminiscent of the smell of catnip. Did you know that catnip isn't just for cats? Historically, it has been grown in medical gardens for human consumption as a sedative and it also works as a mosquito repellent. Smart people reckon that catnip targets a cat's 'happy' (the technical term) receptors in the brain causing them to become very excited, which is followed by a period of mellowness. While a stoned cat is pretty funny, don't let your kitty overindulge. Just like a few too many cattails, too much catnip can make a cat sick.

Ingredients

45ml (1¼fl oz) mezcal
20ml (½fl oz) white vermouth
20ml (½fl oz) crème de menthe
Dash of celery bitters

Instructions

1. Half-fill a mixing glass with ice and add the mezcal, vermouth, crème de menthe and celery bitters.

2. Using a bar spoon, stir the mixture well.

3. Strain into a chilled coupe glass.

Cheshire Cat's Smile

Looking for a unique and colourful cattail? Come down the rabbit hole with me and try this recipe named after the iconic cat from Lewis Carroll's *Alice's Adventures in Wonderland*. For those who don't know, the Cheshire cat is a grinning cat that appears and disappears throughout Alice's journey through Wonderland, sometimes leaving only his famous smile behind when he vanishes. But while Carroll made the character famous, a reference to a grinning Cheshire cat actually appears in writing as early as the 18th century. Wherever the name comes from, the sweet cherry flavours of this cattail are sure to put a smile on any rum lover's face.

Ingredients

50ml (1½fl oz) dark rum
10ml (¼fl oz) dry sherry
10ml (¼fl oz) cherry brandy
Dash of Angostura bitters
1 maraschino cherry, to garnish

Instructions

1. Put an oversized ice cube into a rock glass and add the rum, sherry, cherry liqueur and bitters.
2. Using a bar spoon, stir until the outside of the glass is cool to the touch and the cattail is diluted to your desired strength.
3. Garnish with the cherry.

Curled Up on the Sofa

If you're looking for something to settle down and chill out to while you drink your cattails, peruse this list of my favourite cat-themed films to enjoy. Just be sure to paws if you need to get up and make another drink.

A Street Cat Named Bob: Based on a true story, this emotional feel-good film is the story of James, a homeless addict who turns his life around with the help of his friends, family and a cat named Bob. James and Bob's story is inspirational, beautiful and tear-inducing, so if you're a crier, be warned.

Mary and the Witch's Flower: If you enjoy Japanese animated films, then this is for you. The story of Mary and Peter and Peter's cats, Tib and Gib, is as beautifully animated as it is fantastical. Mary, alone and friendless after moving to a northern English country estate discovers a world of witches and magic. What follows is a journey to uncover truths about her family and herself in order to save Peter and her new feline friends.

Keanu: For those who like comedy, look no further than Keegan-Michael Key and Jordan Peele's hilarious spoof of the hugely successful Keanu Reeves action films. When the girlfriend of Rell, played by Peele, dumps him, he finds a reason to live again in the form of a tiny kitten, Keanu. But Keanu is abducted, so Rell and Clarence, played by Key, must fight tooth and claw if they want to get him back.

Cats: No cat-themed movie list would be complete without this iconic, if very strange, musical adaptation. While it did not receive the best critical reviews, it's worth watching just for the sheer absurdity of seeing world-famous actors (including Judie Dench and Idris Elba) and world-even-famouser musicians (Taylor Swift and Jason Derulo) sing, dance and strut around as half-person, half-animated cats. If you choose to sit down and watch this, be prepared for a very weird evening. Don't say you weren't warned.

The Purrfect Pairs

What's the difference between a Shorthair Cattail and a Purrfect Pair? Well, while the shorthair recipes feature a main spirit and vermouth, Purffect Pairs are what we call duo or trio cattails. Duos are simple cocktails that feature two key elements. Generally, these consist of a 'primary' spirit and a liqueur or secondary spirit. Both are equally important to the flavour or body of the cocktail. Want to make a duo into a trio? Easy, just add that feline favourite - milk or cream.

Purrfect Pairs feature several iconic cocktails. If you love a White Russian or a revolver, you should find cattails in this section worth giving a try. There is also plenty of chance for experimentation here by adding cream, milk or different flavoured liqueurs. But beware, not all duos can become trios and not all trios started life as duos, so try your new recipes yourself before you invite the whole pride round for a tasting. Usually served straight up rather than over ice, these cocktails pack a punch so, as always, enjoy responsibly.

Black
Russian Blue

Named after the dark grey cat (they're not blue don't @ me). This is the Americano of cattails. Dark, bold and not for the faint of heart. Use a high-quality vodka to ensure the taste of coffee really comes through. For those who love coffee and are craving something a bit creamier like an espresso martini, check out the Ragdoll Reviver on page 142.

Ingredients

50ml (1½fl oz) vodka
10ml (¼fl oz) coffee liqueur
Coffee beans, to garnish

Instructions

1. Half-fill a cocktail shaker with ice and add the vodka and coffee liqueur.
2. Shake until well chilled, then strain into a coupe glass.
3. Garnish with coffee beans in the shape of a paw print.

Let Me Out, No Never Mind

Have you ever stood at the door to your house, holding it open, waiting on your stubborn kitten to just make up their goddamn mind? If so, then this cocktail is for you. Based on the revolver (for the door you need installing to keep your cat happy), this is another classic for coffee lovers. The coffee flavours give this a little extra something and keep that bright shine that makes this cattail different to a Mancattan (see page 70). Whiskey lovers, this is a treat.

Ingredients

50ml (1½fl oz) bourbon (a rye-heavy bourbon is recommended)
10ml (¼fl oz) coffee liqueur
2 dashes of orange bitters
Wide strip of orange peel, to garnish

Instructions

1. Half-fill a cocktail shaker with ice and add the bourbon, coffee liqueur and bitters.
2. Shake until well chilled, then strain into a rocks glass.
3. Express the orange peel over the glass, then use it to garnish.

The Cougar

Favoured by the older crowd, I'd recommend this cattail to anyone who's on the prowl. The sweetness of the amaretto offsets the rum beautifully. I'd suggest going for an aged rum if you can find one because, like many things, rum improves and grows more interesting, complex and delicious with age.

Ingredients

50ml (1½fl oz) dark rum
25ml (¾fl oz) amaretto
1 maraschino cherry, to garnish
Dash of Angostura bitters

Instructions

1. Half-fill a cocktail shaker with ice and add the rum and amaretto.
2. Shake until well chilled, then strain into a chilled coupe glass.
3. Garnish with the cherry and finish with a dash of bitters.

KitCat

If you like chocolate, then this cattail is the one for you. Inspired by the famous snappable snack, this drink is perfect for those looking to take a quick break. Grated chocolate gives you so many options to elevate your cattails, and here I've used it twice. First, to rim the martini glass, ensuring you get a chocolaty taste with every mouthful, and second to garnish the cattail for that extra hit of Kit-Katty goodness. To make grating your chocolate easier, I recommend storing it in the refrigerator or freezer for at least an hour before you grate it. That will avoid any messy melting incidents.

Ingredients

25ml (¾fl oz) Cognac or other fine aged brandy
25ml (¾fl oz) dark crème de cacao
25ml (¾fl oz) double (heavy) cream
Grated milk or dark chocolate, to garnish
Freshly grated nutmeg, to garnish

Instructions

1. Rim a martini glass (see page 15) with grated chocolate and set aside in the refrigerator to chill.
2. Half-fill a cocktail shaker with ice and add the Cognac, crème de cacao and cream.
3. Shake well until chilled, then strain into the prepared glass.
4. Garnish with grated nutmeg and more chocolate.

Orangey's White Angel

Inspired by Audrey Hepburn's famous cocktail from *Breakfast at Tiffany's* and named after her cat in the film, Orangey, this cattail is a classic brought back to life for modern cat lovers. Orangey was an animal actor with a prolific career. He worked in film and television from 1951 until 1968, appearing in 10 films and many TV shows and becoming the only cat to win two PATSY awards (Picture Animal Top Star of the Year). Orangey was famously a bit of a grump and was called 'the world's meanest cat' by one studio executive. This cattail takes after him and packs a punch, so don't say you weren't warned.

Ingredients

25ml (¾fl oz) gin
25ml (¾fl oz) vodka

Instructions

1. Half-fill a cocktail shaker with ice and add the gin and vodka.
2. Shake until well chilled, then strain into a chilled coupe glass.

Persian Cream

Cats are all little dudes at heart and this cattail is the dude-iest of them all. Inspired by the White Russian, made famous in the movie *The Big Lebowski*, it's fair to say that nothing ties the room together quite like a gorgeous cat napping on a cosy rug. Just be sure to keep their litter tray clean, to avoid any nihilistic accidents.

Ingredients

50ml (1½fl oz) vodka
25ml (¾fl oz) coffee liqueur
25ml (¾fl oz) double (heavy) cream
White chocolate shavings, to garnish

Instructions

1. Half-fill a cocktail shaker with ice and add the vodka, coffee liqueur and cream.
2. Shake well until chilled, then strain into a rocks glass with ice.
3. Garnish with white chocolate shavings.

Bengal Bramble

Arguably a sour rather than a duo, I've included this cocktail here as the blackberry liqueur is more of a key ingredient than the lemon juice. However, if you're looking for a tangier variant, feel free to add a little more citrus. This cattail is quintessentially British, created in a bar in Soho, London, by legendary mixologist Dick Bradsell and inspired by his experiences picking blackberries from hedgerows on the Isle of White while growing up. If you're feeling extra nostalgic you can muddle together a few blackberries at the bottom of the shaker for extra oomph.

Ingredients

50ml (1½fl oz) gin
25ml (¾fl oz) blackberry liqueur
10ml (¼fl oz) lemon juice (from about ½ lemon)
A few blackberries, to garnish
Lemon wheel, to garnish

Instructions

1. Half-fill a cocktail shaker with ice and add the gin, blackberry liqueur and lemon juice.
2. Shake well to chill, then strain into a chilled coupe glass.
3. Garnish with the blackberries and lemon wheel.

Longhair Varieties

Long, or 'highball', cocktails are made in - you guessed it - a highball glass, by pouring the cocktail over ice and adding soda water, tonic or fruit juice to lengthen the drink. Refreshing, chilled and a bit more 'drinkable', highballs are purrfect for when you've spent too long lounging in the sun or just had a very draining nap. Long drinks is a pretty catch-all category. Ranging from a simple spirit-and-mixer combo to a more complicated drink involving liqueurs, sugars or other aromatics, the key feature is the addition of a non-alcoholic, often fizzy, mixer. For those who love a mojito or Long Island Iced Tea, you've come to the right place.

Longer cocktails have more ways of making and mixing than other types of cattails, as the ingredients vary. Expect to be shaking, stirring, muddling and layering your way to a delicious drink. As they are mostly served over ice, you're also going to want to make sure your freezer is properly stocked in preparation for a cattail-making session. I'd recommend refrigerating your mixers before you make these drinks as well.

Tom Cat Collins

The cattail that gave the highball glass its other name (a collins glass), this has to be one of the most well-known and well-loved highball cattails. Basically a fancy version of a gin and lemonade, this is a refreshing drink that's purrfect for a hot summer's day. Did you know that a Molly is the female equivalent of Tom when talking about cats and can be used to describe any female cat? So, if you'd prefer, help yourself to a Molly Cat Collins.

Ingredients

50ml (1⅔fl oz) gin
25ml (¾fl oz) fresh lemon juice (from about 1 lemon)
10ml (¼fl oz) Simple Syrup (see page 12)
Soda water, to top
Lemon wheel, to garnish
1 maraschino cherry, to garnish

Instructions

1. Fill a highball glass with ice and add the gin,
lemon juice and simple syrup.
2. Top with the soda water, then stir with a bar spoon.
3. Garnish with the lemon wheel and cherry.

Gin Felix

The soufflé of cattails, this recipe is a unique twist on the traditional and refreshing gin fizz. Shaking the 'dry' ingredients for longer creates a stiff foam, then layer the soda water under the foam using a bar spoon and watch your foam rise out of the glass like a perfectly cooked soufflé. Getting this drink right is a great feeling and is sure to impress your friends.

Ingredients

50ml (1½fl oz) gin
25ml (¾fl oz) fresh lemon juice (from about 1 lemon)
10ml (¼fl oz) Simple Syrup (see page 12)
1 medium egg white
Soda water, to top

Instructions

1. Combine the gin, lemon juice, simple syrup and egg white in a cocktail shaker (without ice).

2. Shake vigorously for 3–5 minutes until it forms a thick, foamy emulsion.

3. Add a scoop of ice and shake until well chilled, then strain into a highball glass.

4. Using the reverse of a bar spoon, place the base of the spoon at the bottom of the glass and layer the soda water under the emulsion by slowly pouring the soda water onto the bowl of the spoon. The foam should rise until it is starting to poke out of the top of the glass.

The famous cartoon character Felix the Cat was one of the first animated animals in history, having been created in 1919. His name comes from the similarity between the Latin words for happy (felix) and cat (felis).

Meowjito

Hailing from Cuba, this refreshing, tropical drink is another classic, and is perfect for drinking while reclining on a beach. The origin of this cattail is lost in time, but some stories suggest that it is based on a medicinal drink created by sailors in the employ of Sir Francis Drake. Made with lime, sugar, mint and cane spirit (a precursor to rum) it is supposed to have warded off colds and flu. Wherever it's from, this mix has stood the test of time and is a firm fan favourite. I'd suggest garnishing with a tiny umbrella, but where one isn't available, a lime wedge and sprig of mint will do.

Ingredients

5–8 mint leaves
2 teaspoons granulated sugar
50ml (1½fl oz) white rum
25ml (¾fl oz) fresh lime juice (from about 1 lime)
Soda water, to top
Lime wedge and sprig of mint, to garnish

Instructions

1. Using a muddler, crush the mint and sugar together in the bottom of a highball glass until the aromas of the mint are released.

2. Add a scoop of ice, the rum and lime juice, then top with the soda water.

3. Using a bar spoon, stir until the outside of the glass is cool to the touch.

4. Garnish with the lime wedge and sprig of mint.

Mog Island Mice Tea

OK, which mad person had the idea to combine all these spirits in one drink? It certainly wasn't me. In fact, the origins of this cocktail are as unclear as you'll feel after drinking a couple of them. There are two main competing stories, but my favourite is that the drink was invented by 'Old Man Bishop' (what a great cat name, by the way) during prohibition in the US. The intent was to create a lethal concoction that at first glance appeared to be iced or sweet tea, hence the name. Old Man Bishop then passed the recipe down to his son, who created the modern drink that we know today. Enjoy these carefully. At roughly 22 per cent ABV, they pack a punch.

Ingredients

10ml (¼fl oz) vodka
10ml (¼fl oz) tequila
10ml (¼fl oz) rum
10ml (¼fl oz) gin
10ml (¼fl oz) triple sec
25ml (¾fl oz) fresh lemon juice
25ml (¾fl oz) Simple Syrup (see page 12)
Cola, to top
Lemon wheel, to garnish

Instructions

1. Half-fill a cocktail shaker with ice and add the vodka, tequila, rum, gin, triple sec, lemon juice and simple syrup.
2. Shake until well chilled, then strain into a highball glass with some ice.
3. Top with the cola and garnish with the lemon wheel.

Dark 'n' Scratchy

Tropical drinks make up a large proportion of the more famous long cattails out there, and this recipe is no exception. The original was named by a sailor in the Caribbean for its colour. The dark rum reminded him of the sudden storm clouds that could form over the warm seas, surprising sailors and forcing them to search out safe harbour. Mine is named after a similar feeling - that moment when you hear your cat attacking the sofa and must desperately dash across the house to try to save your furniture. No, Mittens! Not the Chesterfield!

Ingredients

50ml (1½fl oz) dark rum
Ginger beer, to top
Lime wedge, to garnish

Instructions

1. Fill a highball glass with ice and add the rum.
2. Top with the ginger beer, then stir well with a bar spoon.
3. Garnish with the lime wedge.

Moscow Mew

One may ask why this cattail is served in a copper mug rather than a normal glass. The answer you might get is that it's tradition. It's aesthetic. It's just like, you know, the way it's done, man. While these are all valid answers, there is actually a more functional reason. As copper is a good conductor, it takes on the temperature of the cocktail. Combined with a handle that stops you from touching the mug directly, this keeps the cocktail colder, helping to enhance the flavours of the vodka. So now you know. Curiosity can sometimes be a very useful quality.

Ingredients

50ml (1½fl oz) vodka
125ml (4fl oz/½ cup) ginger beer
10ml (¼fl oz) fresh lime juice (from about ½ lime)
Lime wheel, to garnish

Instructions

1. Fill a copper mug with ice and add the vodka, ginger beer and lime juice. If you don't have a copper mug available, a highball glass works well.
2. Stir well with a bar spoon, then garnish with the lime wheel.

Feline Colada

This is an unusual cocktail for cat lovers, as it's frequently favoured by those who enjoy getting caught in the rain. Inspired by the piña colada, this frozen cattail will have you reconsidering your daily 'big stretch' regime and instead have you answering lonely heart ads in the local paper. The tropical flavours of the pineapple juice and coconut cream give this drink a real 'holiday' feel, making it great for anyone with a sweet tooth. In this recipe, the ice is blended with the drink to create a smoothie- or slushy-like experience. If you don't have a blender to hand you can mix a version on the rocks or with crushed ice. Simply add the ingredients to a cocktail shaker with ice, then strain into a highball glass over ice.

Ingredients

50ml (1½fl oz) white rum
75ml (2½fl oz) pineapple juice
25ml (¾fl oz) coconut cream
Pineapple wedge, to garnish
1 maraschino cherry, to garnish

Instructions

1. Add a cup of ice (5–8 cubes) to a blender with the rum, pineapple juice and coconut cream.
2. Blend until you have a smooth, slushy-like consistency.
3. Pour into a hurricane glass and garnish with the pineapple wedge.

Sam's Bloody Mary

Famed pop artist Andy Warhol kept 25 cats over his lifetime. And while the feline fancier was undoubtedly creative with his art, the naming of his kittens was less so. Every cat, save one, was named Sam. So, in these kittens' honour, and because of Andy's love of tomatoes and soup, I've named this cattail recipe after Warhol's many Sams. While this is a classic boozy brunch recipe, did you know that tomato juice is also hugely popular on aeroplanes? German airline Lufthansa discovered they were serving over 200,000 litres (53,000 gallons) a year. Something about the sweet and savoury taste hits just the right spot at forty thousand feet.

Ingredients

50ml (1½fl oz) vodka
125ml (4fl oz/½ cup) tomato juice
10ml (¼fl oz) fresh lemon juice (from about ½ lime)
2 dashes of Worcestershire sauce
4 dashes of Tabasco sauce
Pinch of salt and pepper
Celery stalk, to garnish
Lemon wheel, to garnish

Instructions

1. Half-fill a mixing glass with ice and add the vodka, tomato juice, lemon juice, Worcestershire sauce, Tabasco sauce, salt and pepper.

2. Using a bar spoon, stir until the outside of the shaker is cool to the touch.

3. Strain into a highball glass with ice, then garnish with the celery stalk and lemon wheel.

4. Season to taste with more salt, pepper and Tabasco as needed.

112

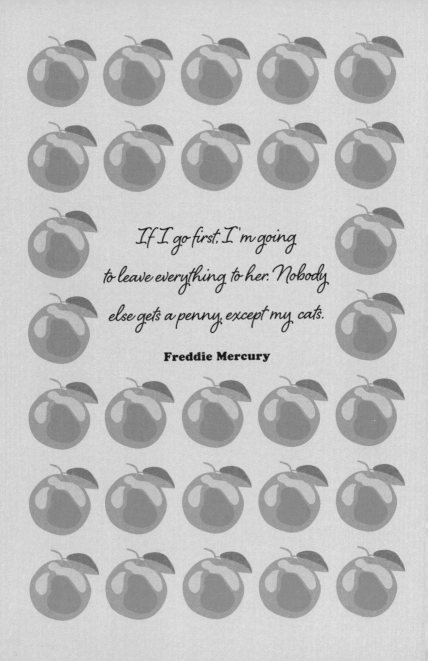

If I go first, I'm going to leave everything to her. Nobody else gets a penny, except my cats.

Freddie Mercury

Queen

This cattail is a variation on the classic vodka tonic, favourite drink of world-changing musician and cat-lover Freddie Mercury. Mercury adopted many cats throughout his life, all of whom lived with him in his house in London. At one point, he had more than ten and each had its own Christmas stocking filled with treats and toys. He'd even call them while on tour, asking his friend to hold the phone up to each cat so he could talk to them from his hotel room. In 1985 he dedicated a solo album, *Mr Bad Guy* to his cats, with the note: 'To my cat Jerry—also Tom, Oscar, and Tiffany, and all the cat lovers across the universe—screw everybody else!'

Ingredients

50ml (1½fl oz) vodka
1 teaspoon orange marmalade
25ml (¾fl oz) freshly brewed Earl Grey tea, cooled
Tonic water, to top

Instructions

1. Half-fill a cocktail shaker with ice and add the vodka, marmalade and tea.
2. Shake until well chilled, then strain into a highball glass with ice.
3. Top with the tonic and stir with a bar spoon to combine.

Olivia Benson, Meredith Grey and Benjamin Button

Named after the cats of world-famous pop star Taylor Swift, this cattail is inspired by her favourite drink, the vodka diet Coke. I've spiced it up with a little lime, to offset the flavours and help the drink really purr. Fun fact, because of the commercial work that Olivia Benson has done with Swift, the 2023 Pet Rich List estimates her net worth to be approximately $97 million (£79 million). For all of you reading who have just had a sudden realization that a cat is richer than you will ever be... enjoy your existential crisis.

Ingredients

50ml (1½fl oz) vodka
Diet cola, to top
Lime wedge, to garnish

Instructions

1. Fill a highball glass with ice, then add the vodka and top with the diet cola.
2. Stir with a bar spoon, then garnish with the lime wedge.

A Night on the Cat Nip

If you're in the party mood, perhaps a cat-themed drinking game would suit your cattail gathering. I've set out the rules for one below. While experiences may vary (good luck getting any self-respecting cat to cooperate with a human's idea of what it should do) hopefully these ideas will give you a good starting point.

Rules

Cat on the lap: If a cat chooses to sit on someone's lap during the evening, that person may not move for any reason until the cat has chosen to depart. If they need to move, they must take a drink.

Cat names: For the duration of the game, every participant must have a 'cat name', decided on by the other participants. Some suggestions include: Fluffy, Muffin, Kitty, Mr Furballs and Socks. Everyone must refer to that person only by their cat name, and if they don't, they must take a drink.

Risky drinks: Cats will knock anything off the table given a chance, so during the game you need to be careful not to leave any drinks too close to a table edge. Any drinks that are left within two paws width (a distance agreed upon at the beginning of the game) of the edge of a table or counter are deemed 'risky' and the offender must take a drink.

No thumbs: Cats don't have thumbs, so all drinking throughout the evening must be done without opposable thumbs. Anyone caught holding a drink in an un-catlike manner must take another drink.

Slow blink: Cats show affection and trust through a slow blink, demonstrating that they feel safe enough to close their eyes around you. You and your friends should also be able to show this trust and respect to each other. At any time, one player may make eye contact with another and slow blink at them. If the other player doesn't return the blink, then they must take a drink.

Feel free to add to these rules. I feel they make a great addition to any cocktail evening – just be sure to enjoy your cattails responsibly.

Exotic
Breeds

Congratulations, you've made it to the Exotic Breeds. By now, I'm going to assume that this isn't the first cattail you've mixed. If so, and you're looking to try some more complicated recipes with far-flung ingredients, then this is the chapter for you.

These cattails feature one or more unusual ingredients. Where possible, I've tried to include options and alternatives in case you can't get your hands on the right ingredients, but part of the fun of these drinks is experimenting with new and unique tastes. It's worth roaming a bit further afield and hunting out the ingredients where you can. Each drink is named after a cat breed or famous cat that links back to the unique ingredient, so enjoy a bit of cat trivia while you mix your drinks. There are ingredients and flavours from all over the world, so hop in your cat carrier and enjoy the ride.

Winter in Maine Coon

Maine Coons first originated in the northeast of the USA. Winters there are very cold, and the Maine Coons' long hair and thick fur made them great at braving the temperatures outside. Sometimes called the dogs of the cat world (though why anyone thinks that's a compliment is beyond me), Maine Coons are known for their intelligence and active and playful nature. That makes them the perfect kitty to represent this cocktail. Featuring the sweetness of Maine from the maple syrup, this warm and cosy drink is perfect for enjoying next to a roaring fire while snow falls outside.

Ingredients

50ml (1½fl oz) bourbon
25ml (¾fl oz) sweet vermouth
10ml (¼fl oz) maple syrup
2 dashes of orange bitters
1 maraschino cherry, to garnish
Strip of orange peel, to garnish

Instructions

1. Half-fill a cocktail shaker with ice and add the bourbon, sweet vermouth, maple syrup and bitters.

2. Shake until well chilled, then strain into a rocks glass with an oversized ice cube.

3. Express the orange peel over the glass, then use it to garnish. Finally, add the maraschino cherry.

A Scottish Fold

Made with two authentic Scottish ingredients, this cattail brings to mind visions of the Highlands and the sound of bagpipes. The first ingredient, Scotch whisky, can only be produced in Scotland, must be matured for a minimum of three years in oak barrels and can have no added sweeteners or flavourings. Some of the most famous Scotches go for over £7,800 ($10,000) a bottle. The second ingredient, Drambuie, is a liqueur made from Scotch, heather honey and a mixture of herbs and spices. The recipe supposedly dates back to 1746, when Charles Edward Stuart (aka Bonnie Prince Charlie) fled to the Isle of Skye after a battle with the English and was gifted the recipe by a boat captain.

Ingredients

10ml (¼fl oz) hot water
10ml (¼fl oz) honey
50ml (1½fl oz) Scotch
10ml (¼fl oz) Drambuie
25ml (¾fl oz) fresh lemon juice (from about 1 lemon)

Instructions

1. Prepare the honey syrup by mixing the hot water and honey together until the honey has dissolved. You can save any unused syrup for use in later cocktails.
2. Put an oversized ice cube into a rocks glass and add the Scotch, Drambuie, lemon juice and 10ml (¼fl oz) of the honey syrup.
3. Using a bar spoon, stir until the outside of the glass is cool to the touch and the cattail is diluted to your desired strength.

Cleocatra

This next cattail is inspired by the great cats of Egypt. Did you know that recent research estimates that the Great Sphinx of Giza was built over 9,000 years ago? This drink uses sahlab, a Middle Eastern milk-based drink that we know cats would love if they could get their hands on it. I would not recommend giving it to them, though. Adult cats are actually lactose intolerant, so unless you want a messy litter box, stay well away. Store any leftover sahlab in the fridge for up to 3 days.

Ingredients

50ml (1½fl oz) rye whiskey
100ml (3½fl oz/scant ½ cup) sahlab, chilled (see below)
10ml (¼fl oz) Honey Syrup (see page 124)
¼ teaspoon vanilla extract
Cinnamon stick, to garnish
Star anise, to garnish

For the sahlab
250ml (8fl oz/1 cup) whole (full-fat) milk
250ml (8fl oz/1 cup) double (heavy) cream
50g (1¾ oz/¼ cup) granulated sugar
15g (½ oz) sahlab powder
1 teaspoon rose water

Instructions

1. First, prepare the sahlab. Heat the milk and cream in a saucepan over a medium heat until warm but not boiling.
2. Add the sugar and sahlab powder and whisk constantly until the sugar and powder have dissolved and the mixture is just about to boil.
3. Remove from the heat and add the rose water, then set aside to cool before transferring to the refrigerator to chill.
4. Half-fill a cocktail shaker with ice and add the whiskey, sahlab, honey syrup and vanilla extract.
5. Shaked until well chilled, then strain into a highball glass with ice.
6. Garnish with the cinnamon stick and star anise.

Havana Brown

The Havana Brown is a unique breed of cat with a beautiful dark brown coat, which is the result of a planned breeding program between Siamese and black cats by British Siamese cat owners. The cat's colouring has inspired this rum- and coffee-flavoured cocktail. The chocolaty liqueur and garnish add a sweetness that offsets the bitter coffee taste. Great for mocha and rum lovers alike. For an added kitty kick, use a stencil shaped like a cat's paw or tail for your garnish.

Ingredients

50ml (1½fl oz) aged Cuban dark rum
25ml (¾fl oz) coffee liqueur
10ml (¼fl oz) crème de cacao
175ml (2½fl oz) double (heavy) cream
Milk chocolate shavings, to garnish

Instructions

1. Half-fill a cocktail shaker with ice and add the rum, coffee liqueur, crème de cacao and cream.

2. Shake until well chilled, then strain into a martini glass.

3. Garnish with the chocolate shavings.

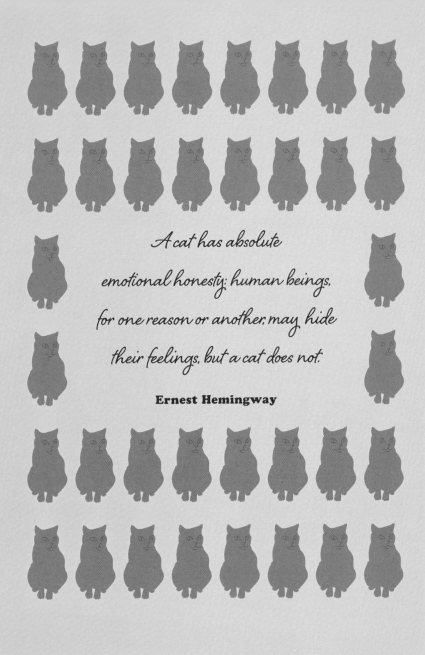

A cat has absolute
emotional honesty: human beings,
for one reason or another, may hide
their feelings, but a cat does not.

Ernest Hemingway

Nap in
the Afternoon

Ernest Hemingway loved cats. Quoted as saying, 'One cat just leads to another', he fostered many kitties including a polydactyl white cat named Snow White. Polydactyl cats have six toes rather than the more regular five toes on the front feet and four on the back. The Ernest Hemingway Home and Museum is now home to roughly 60 polydactyl kittens, many of which are descended from Snow White. This cattail is inspired by Hemingway's favourite drink - a mixture of absinthe and Champagne named 'Death in the Afternoon'. Please enjoy more responsibly than Hemingway famously did.

Ingredients

30ml (1fl oz) absinthe
120ml (4fl oz/½ cup) Champagne

Instructions

1. Combine the absinthe and Champagne
in a Champagne glass.

Builders' Brew

The traditional British cup of tea. A sign of friendship and hospitality. The start
of a moment shared, or a peace offering when things haven't been working out. There are
so many uses for the cup of tea, and now, we're going to make it into a cattail. This very
British drink features the fragrance of gin and Earl Grey tea combined with fresh lemon
and mellow honey. While I'm normally against putting honey in tea, I'll make the
exception for this cattail. If you want to take your heart to heart to
the next level, try this.

Ingredients

50ml (1½fl oz) gin
25ml (¾fl oz) freshly brewed Earl Grey tea, chilled
25ml (¾fl oz) fresh lemon juice (from about 1 lemon)
10ml (¼fl oz) Honey Syrup (see page 124)
Lemon twist, to garnish
Earl Grey tea leaves, to garnish (optional)

Instructions

1. Put an oversized ice cube into a rocks glass and
add the gin, tea, lemon juice and honey syrup.
2. Using a bar spoon, stir until the outside of the
glass is cool to the touch.
3. Express the lemon twist over the glass, then use it to
garnish along with the tea leaves, if using.

Oriental Shorthair

A very unusual cat, the Oriental Shorthair is noticeable by her large ears, angular face and long, slender frame. These cats are very chatty and love a bit of human company. I've tried to honour their unique spirit in this cattail, which features sake and lychee liqueur as the key ingredients. While sake is frequently called 'rice wine', it's actually made in a brewing process closer to that of beer, where the starch is converted into sugars and fermented. Sake can be drunk hot or cold, but I'd stick with cold sake for this cattail. Lychee liqueur is a less common type of liqueur, but should be available online or in larger supermarkets. Made from the sweet fruit that originates from Vietnam, India and other South Asian countries, its unique flavour makes for a great addition to this cattail.

Ingredients

50ml (1½fl oz) sake
25ml (¾fl oz) lychee liqueur
25ml (¾fl oz) fresh lime juice (from about 1 lime)
25ml Simple Syrup (see page 12)
Splash of Champagne
1 tinned lychee, to garnish
Lime twist, to garnish

Instructions

1. Half-fill a cocktail shaker with ice and add the sake, lychee liqueur, lime juice and simple syrup.
2. Shake until well child, then strain into a Champagne glass and top with the Champagne.
3. Garnish with the lychee and lime twist.

Catterina's Dinner

While this is a book about cats and cocktails, not ravens, it would be remiss of me not to mention Edgar Allen Poe. While better known for his dark poetry and for inspiring Eurovision songs, Poe also kept a tortoiseshell cat named Catterina. This classic eggnog recipe is inspired by Poe's love of brandy and the winter drink of which it is a key ingredient. I also think Catterina would have enjoyed this recipe with lots of milk, eggs and cream. It makes enough for six people, because who wants to make eggnog for only themselves.

Serves 6

Ingredients

6 large eggs, separated
150g (5½oz/generous ⅔ cup) granulated sugar
240ml (8fl oz/1 cup) double (heavy) cream
480ml (16fl oz/2 cups) whole (full-fat) milk
½ teaspoon ground nutmeg, plus extra to garnish
180ml (6fl oz/¾ cup) brandy
1 teaspoon vanilla extract
Cinnamon sticks, to garnish

Instructions

1. In a bowl, whisk together the egg yolks and sugar until the mixture is smooth and creamy.

2. Combine the cream, milk and nutmeg in a saucepan over a medium heat and heat until hot but not boiling. Once hot, remove from the heat.

3. Slowly add a small amount of the hot milk mixture to the egg yolks, whisking continuously. This is called tempering and prevents the eggs from scrambling. Continue to slowly add the milk mixture until everything is combined.

4. Pour the mixture back into the saucepan and cook over medium-low heat for about 5 minutes, stirring continuously until it has thickened and coats the back of a spoon.

5. Remove the mixture from the heat and let it cool for a few minutes, then stir in the brandy and vanilla extract.

6. In a separate bowl, use a hand-held electric whisk to whisk the egg whites until stiff peaks form. Gently fold this into the milk and egg yolk mixture until combined.

7. Allow the mixture to cool at room temperature before transferring to the refrigerator. Chill for at least 4 hours, or preferably overnight.

8. When you're ready to serve, pour the eggnog into glasses. Garnish with more nutmeg and a cinnamon stick.

Abyssinia

Ethiopia was once known in Europe as Abyssinia, a name shared with a unique cat breed. These slender cats have a distinctive 'ticked' tabby coat, with kittens featuring different banded colourings. However, while the cats are named Abyssinia, they do not actually originate from Ethiopia. Genetic studies instead show that the cats originated from the coast of the Indian Ocean and parts of Southeast Asia. The name is thought to have come about as the cats were first exhibited in England after being imported from Ethiopia. The name has stuck, and so I've used it as the inspiration for our next cattail. Featuring an Ethiopian honey wine similar to mead called *tej*, this warm and sweet cattail is great for supping on while snoozing on a sunny terrace with your feline friend.

Ingredients

50ml (1½fl oz) tej (or other sweet mead)
25ml (¾fl oz) spiced rum
25ml (¾fl oz) fresh lemon juice (from about 1 lemon)
Dash of Angostura bitters
10ml (¼fl oz) Honey Syrup (see page 124)
Lemon twist, to garnish

Instructions

1. Half-fill a cocktail shaker with ice and add the tej, rum, lemon juice, bitters and honey syrup.

2. Shake until well chilled, then strain into a rocks glass with an oversized ice cube.

3. Garnish with the lemon twist.

A Spicy Aztec

Purportedly a now-extinct breed of cat, the Aztec or Mexican Hairless Cat
was a very unusual breed. Originating only from Mexico, these small kitties were not
totally hairless, as they would grow a thin coat of light fur along their back and tail in the
winter. Unsurprisingly, they loved a warm body to cuddle up against when not basking in
the warm sun of their homeland. This love of heat has also inspired this spicy cattail.
Made with chilli-infused triple sec, it packs a serious punch. For those who don't enjoy
spice, mix with care. You may want to add extra cucumber and coriander
(cilantro) to the recipe to offset the heat.

Ingredients

3 slices of cucumber
2 stalks of coriander (cilantro)
75ml (2½fl oz) mezcal
25ml (¾fl oz) serrano-infused triple sec (see below)
75ml (2½fl oz) fresh lime juice (from about 3 limes)
25ml (¾fl oz) agave nectar

For the serrano-infused triple sec
1 litre (34fl oz/4¼ cups) triple sec
100g (3½ oz) serrano chillies, chopped and frozen

To garnish
Flaky sea salt and granulated sugar
Lime slices
Sliced chillies

Instructions

1. First, make the serrano-infused triple sec. Pour the triple sec into a glass or stainless-steel container and add the frozen chillies.

2. Leave to steep at room temperature, tasting every 20 minutes or so, until it reaches your desired heat level. I recommend around 1½ hours.

3. Strain the triple sec and transfer to a bottle or jar, then store in the refrigerator (it will last for months).

4. When you're ready to make the cocktail, rim a highball glass with an equal mixture of salt and sugar (see page 15) and fill with ice.

5. Using a muddler, crush the cucumber and coriander in the bottom of the glass until aromatic.

6. Half-fill a cocktail shaker with ice and add the mezcal, infused triple sec, lime juice and agave nectar. Shake until well chilled, then strain into the prepared glass.

7. Using a bar spoon, stir the cocktail to infuse the drink with the muddled aromatics.

8. Garnish with the lime slice and chilli.

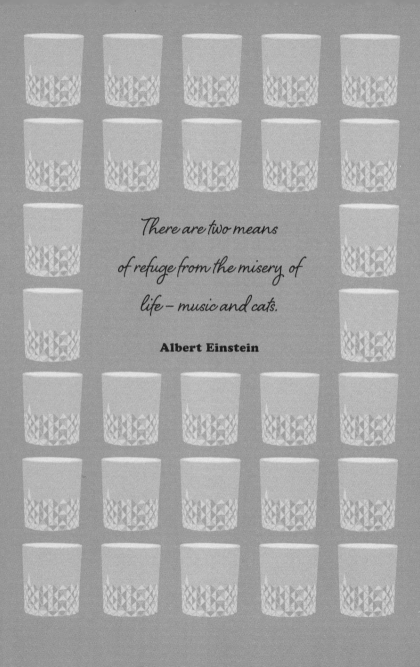

There are two means
of refuge from the misery of
life – music and cats.

Albert Einstein

T=MC²

Did you know that as well as being a world-renowned physicist and all-round smart guy, Albert Einstein also made great choices in pets. His tabby cat, Tiger, was one of his greatest companions. Now, if Albert could have also discovered a way to stop my cat scratching my sofa, that would really have been something. This drink is inspired by Einstein and Tiger. Einstein wasn't much of a drinker, but he smoked like a chimney, so I've gone for smoky mezcal and a flaming orange to help bring this drink to life. The orange is a great party trick and is sure to blow your guests' minds, just like trying to understand general relativity.

Ingredients

25ml (¾fl oz) mezcal
10ml (¼fl oz) Campari
10ml (¼fl oz) Cynar
25ml (¾fl oz) vermouth rosso
2 drops of Scrappy's Black Lemon Bitters
Wide strip of orange peel, to garnish

Instructions

1. Put an oversized ice cube into a rocks glass and add the mezcal, Campari, Cynar and vermouth.

2. Using a bar spoon, stir until the outside of the glass is cool to the touch, then add the bitters and allow to infuse into the cattail.

3. To flame the orange, hold the orange peel 2–3cm (¾–1¼ inches) away from a burning match. Express the oils from the orange towards the match and watch them light up and catch fire with a big flash. Your friends will be wowed.

4. Garnish with the orange peel.

Ragdoll Reviver

This peppy cattail is based on every bartender's favourite drink to make (try ordering a round of these on a busy Friday night and see what happens). With over eight ingredients, including fresh espresso, you can probably see why. However, don't let that put you off trying this recipe at home, especially since it was inspired in part by my very own cat. A ragdoll with beautiful blue eyes, there is nothing that helps me get out of bed more than him trying to bite my toes in the morning because he wants breakfast. So, in honour of him, and his... assertive tendencies... try this drink and enjoy the zoomies that it hopefully gives you.

Ingredients

50ml (1½fl oz) vanilla vodka
25ml (¾fl oz) Baileys Irish Cream
25ml (¾fl oz) chilled espresso
25ml (¾fl oz) coffee liqueur
10ml (¼fl oz) double (heavy) cream
Dash of blue curaçao
Dark chocolate shavings, to garnish
Edible blue glitter, to garnish

Instructions

1. Half-fill a cocktail shaker with ice and add the vodka, Baileys, espresso, coffee liqueur and cream.
2. Shake until well chilled, then strain into a martini glass.
3. Add a few drops of blue curaçao to the top of the cocktail to echo a ragdoll's eyes.
4. Garnish with the shaved chocolate and edible blue glitter.

Kittens' Mogtails

If you don't drink, aren't drinking or just don't fancy a drink right now, this chapter is for you. While any of the cattails in this book can be made using alcohol-free versions of the base spirits, the recipes in this chapter aim to be naturally non-alcoholic, with no spirits at all. Also knowns as 'zero-proof' drinks, mocktails rose to fame alongside their alcohol filled cousins. The word was first listed in the dictionary in 1916. Since then, Mogtails have been on the up and up, though interestingly they were not as popular during the Prohibition era. The recent rise of spin classes and healthy eating has led to a major surge in their popularity, with bars serving only alcohol-free drinks popping up all over the place. While I might be a bit annoyed if I accidentally turned up at one of these bars without foreknowledge, it's good to know there are options for every taste. Great for kittens, mums to be or maybe someone who had a bit of a heavy night last night. Try these different fruity and flavourful recipes and see which you prefer.

Garfield's Mondays

Inspired by the orange cartoon cat himself, this mogtail pairs fantastically with lasagne. The orangey-red colour of the drink should remind you of Garfield's tabby coat and tastes a little like a negroni. This is the perfect recipe to brighten your Monday without putting undue stress on the rest of the week.

Ingredients

25ml (¾fl oz) citrus syrup (see below)
25ml (¾fl oz) white grape juice
Orange slice, to garnish

For the citrus syrup
250g (9oz/generous 1 cup) caster (superfine) sugar
250ml (8fl oz/1 cup) boiling water
1 grapefruit, peeled and finely chopped
3 slices of orange
6 cardamom pods, lightly crushed
Pinch of ground coriander

Instructions

1. First, make the syrup. Combine all the ingredients in a saucepan over a medium heat and simmer for 5 minutes.
2. Once soft, crush the fruit with the back of a spoon to release the juices, then remove from the heat.
3. Leave the syrup to cool, then strain and discard the leftover fruit pieces. Store any unused syrup in the refrigerator for use in later mogtails (it will last for months).
4. When you're ready to make the mogtail, put an oversized ice cube into a rocks glass and add the syrup and grape juice
5. Using a bar spoon, stir until the outside of the glass is cool to the touch.
6. Garnish with the orange slice.

Aristocats' Tipple

Inspired by the famous cartoon cats, it felt wrong to name an alcoholic drink after these childhood throwbacks. So here they are instead, lending their name to this sweet and smooth drink. I can see the Duchess sipping on one of these from a large saucer. Just a word of warning, avoid this if you're pregnant. While unlikely, unpasteurized egg whites do present a risk to you and your baby.

Ingredients

100ml (3½fl oz/scant ½ cup) pineapple juice
50ml (1½fl oz) lemon juice
1 medium egg white
Dash of almond extract
10ml (¼fl oz) maraschino cherry syrup (or more if you prefer)
A few maraschino cherries, to garnish

Instructions

1. Combine the pineapple juice, lemon juice, egg white, almond extract and cherry syrup in a cocktail shaker (with no ice).
2. Shake vigorously for 3–5 minutes until it forms a thick, foamy emulsion.
3. Add a scoop of ice and shake again until chilled, then strain the mixture into a coupe glass.
4. Garnish with the maraschino cherries.

Momma's Milk

This wouldn't be a kitten section if we didn't have a milk-based mogtail, so ta-da! Enjoy this deliciously creamy and vanilla-y drink. Most cats are actually lactose intolerant, however - so where does the idea come from that cat's love milk? Well, it comes from farm cats, who got a taste for the fresh, fatty, sweet milk of just-milked cows. Unfortunately, just because you like something, doesn't mean it's good for you. For a variation, try blending the ice with the drink rather than straining. You'll end up with a frappé-style beverage, best enjoyed through a wide straw. This way you don't have to leave the house for your favourite coffee shop beverages and can spend even more time with your kittens. Use a cat stencil when garnishing for an extra feline effect.

Ingredients

250ml (8fl oz/1 cup) milk (whole/full-fat, skimmed or an alternative milk, depending on your preference)
125ml (4fl oz/½ cup) double (heavy) cream (optional)
15ml (½fl oz) Simple Syrup (or to taste; see page 12)
1 teaspoon vanilla extract
Cocoa powder or chocolate shavings, to garnish

Instructions

1. Half-fill a cocktail shaker with ice and add the milk, cream, if using, syrup and vanilla extract.
2. Shake until well chilled, then strain into a highball glass.
3. Garnish with the cocoa powder or chocolate shavings.

Mewjit-no

No points for guessing which drink this is an alcohol-free version of, I'm afraid.
But while obvious, that doesn't make this mogtail any less delicious. Perfect for any hot
summer's day, this drink is as tasty as it is refreshing. The mint and lime pair so well
together. Like cats and string, or cats and cuddles, or cats and... you get the idea.

Ingredients

2 teaspoons granulated sugar
5–8 mint leaves
30ml fresh lime juice (from about 1 lime)
Soda water, to top
Lime wedge, to garnish

Instructions

1. Using a muddler, crush the sugar and mint in a highball
glass, then add ice to chill.
2. Add the lime juice and soda water, then stir with a bar
spoon until the sugar has dissolved.
3. Garnish with the lime wedge.

Frozen Choupette

For those who don't know, Choupette was the adored pet cat of the late
Karl Lagerfeld (the world-famous fashion designer). But oh, she is so much more. An
icon, a muse, an inspiration, this Birman is famous the world over. She has over 46,000
fans on the Twitter page created in her honour and has been 'interviewed' by various
fashion magazines. Recently, she was immortalized during the 2023 Met Gala. The theme
celebrated Lagerfeld's life and work and inspired Jared Leto to wear a life-sized, full-body
Choupette costume. While Choupette couldn't attend herself, if she'd been there, I'm sure
she would have had a drink just like this alcohol-free frozen piña colada.

Ingredients

125ml (4 fl oz/½ cup) pineapple juice
75ml (2½fl oz) coconut cream
Pineapple wedge, to garnish

Instructions

1. Add a cup of ice (5–8 cubes) to a blender with
the pineapple juice and coconut cream.
2. Blend until you have a smooth, slushy-like consistency.
3. Pour into a highball glass and garnish with
the pineapple wedge.

Pink Panther

This mogtail is a total steal. Inspired by the films and later animated character, make sure you keep track of where you put this mogtail down, otherwise it might not be there when you next look. Originally the Pink Panther was a diamond rather than a cat, but the series has now evolved and the panther is known worldwide. His light-fingered touch makes this delicate and refreshing mogtail the perfect drink to finish our collection with.

Ingredients

125ml (4 fl oz/½ cup) watermelon juice
75ml (2½fl oz) fresh lemon juice (from about 2 lemons)
50ml (1½fl oz) Simple Syrup (see page 12)
Soda water, to top
Lemon wheel, to garnish
Watermelon slice, to garnish

Instructions

1. Fill a highball glass with ice and add the watermelon juice, lemon juice and simple syrup.

2. Top with the soda water, then stir with a bar spoon until chilled.

3. Garnish with the lemon wheel and watermelon slice.

Index

A big thank you to all of the beautiful kitties who contributed their portraits for this book: Olive, Peep, Salvador, Buster, Bert, Winnie, Cuddles, Cleo, Tully, Cornflake, Scott, the Shalaby cats, Momo, Pel, Missy, Massimo and Mushu.

First published in Great Britain in 2024 by Greenfinch
An imprint of Quercus Editions Ltd
Carmelite House
50 Victoria Embankment
London
EC4Y 0DZ

An Hachette UK company

HB ISBN 978-1-52943-569-6

eBook ISBN 978-1-52943-570-2

10 9 8 7 6 5 4 3 2

Commissioned by Emily Arbis
Project managed by Lucy Kingett
Text by Mark Davison
Illustrations by Lorna Syson
Design by Tokiko Morishima and Ginny Zeal

Printed and bound in China

MIX
Paper | Supporting
responsible forestry
FSC® C016973
FSC
www.fsc.org

Papers used by Greenfinch are from well-managed forests and other responsible sources.